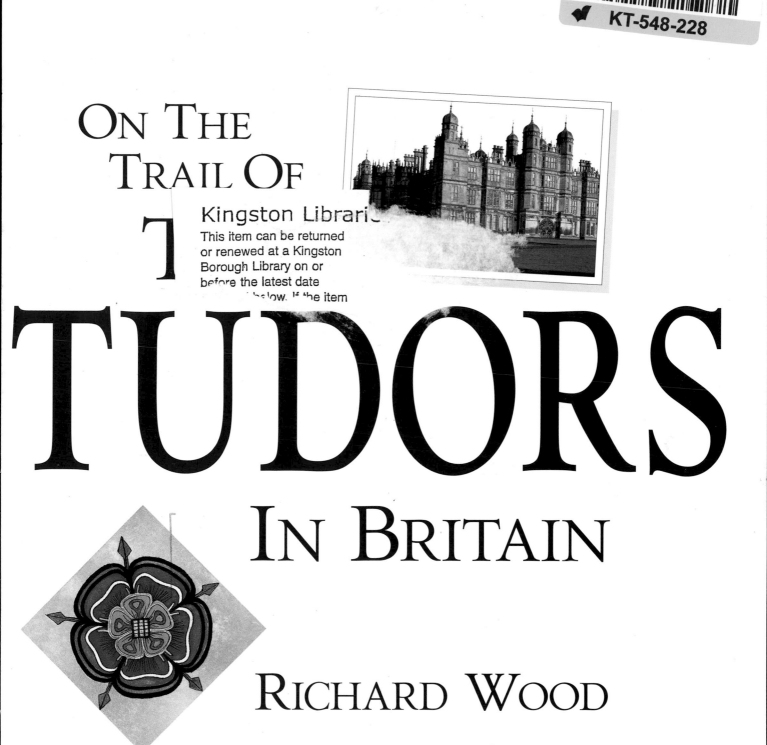

ON THE TRAIL OF THE TUDORS

IN BRITAIN

RICHARD WOOD

FRANKLIN WATTS
LONDON • SYDNEY

© 1999 Franklin Watts
First published in Great Britain by
Franklin Watts
96 Leonard Street
London EC2A 4XD

Franklin Watts Australia
14 Mars Road
Lane Cove
NSW 2006
Australia

ISBN 0 7496 3229 1 HB
ISBN 0 7496 3590 8 PB

Dewey Decimal Classification 942.05
A CIP record for this book is available
from the British Library

Printed in Dubai, U.A.E.

Planning and production by Discovery Books Ltd
Editor: Helena Attlee
Design: Simon Borrough
Consultant: Tim Copeland
Art: Stuart Carter, Stefan Chabluk

Photographs: All pictures by Alex Ramsay except:
page 4: A Palace Interior with Ladies and
Gentlemen Dancing and Playing Music (oil on
panel) by Louis de Caullery (c.1580-1621) Rafael
Valls Gallery, London/ Bridgeman Art Library
London/New York; Mary Evans Picture Library:
page 24; Richard Kalina: page 27; The National
Trust Photo Library: pages 12 (Andrew
Van Einsiedel), 15 (John Bethnell), 14 (Andrew
Van Einsiedel); Mary Rose Trust: 18 (both), 19
(top); John Tramper: page 26; The Weald and
Downland Museum: pages 8, 17; Richard Wood:
page 9.

CONTENTS

Who Were the Tudors?

In 1485, Henry Tudor defeated and killed the unpopular King Richard III at the Battle of Bosworth.

The year 1485 marks a new chapter in the history of Britain - the end of the Middle Ages and the start of Tudor times. The late Middle Ages had been a time of great unrest in Britain. When Henry Tudor became King Henry VII, he brought peace to the land. With peace came wealth. Now that merchants could travel safely, trade flourished and money from taxes, loans and fines began to pour into the royal coffers.

These simple early Tudor furnishings at Stokesay Castle, Shropshire, were hand-made in oak by skilled joiners.

Henry VII's descendants followed in his footsteps. During 118 years of Tudor rule, England became richer than ever before. As the country became wealthier, towns grew, beautiful houses were built and schools and colleges were set up. Arts and crafts flourished, too. England was home to great painters, writers and musicians.

You will not have to travel far to begin your Tudor trail - the evidence of Tudor times is all around us.

TUDOR CLOTHES

The clothes of wealthy Tudor men and women were decorated with jewels and embroidered with gold thread. Middle-class people, like traders and craftsmen, wore plainer versions of these rich costumes. Poor people had to make do with simple, loose-fitting clothes made from woollen cloth. The cloth was usually dyed brown or blue with vegetable dyes.

▲ An entertainment being performed in an Elizabethan palace. Under their clothes, the ladies wore wire cages called farthingales. This gave their dresses a fashionable shape.

▼ The decorative stone work of Burghley House in Lincolnshire, England's largest Tudor mansion, was designed to show off the wealth of its owner.

TUDOR TOWNS

Under Tudor rule England became a more peaceful and prosperous place. During this period, trade was profitable and many towns grew rich.

In Lavenham, Suffolk, you can easily imagine what a typical Tudor town was like. The fine Tudor houses, large church and beautiful Guildhall tell us that Lavenham was once a very wealthy town. The rich merchants of Lavenham made their money from selling wool and woollen cloth.

Records show that the money for building the church and the Guildhall was paid by local wool merchants. The Guildhall was used as a meeting place by merchants and weavers. They met to agree on wages and prices, to check the quality of cloth and to arrange for the care of sick or elderly workers.

Most of the houses on this Lavenham street date from early Tudor times. Jutting out upper floors, called jetties, were very fashionable in Tudor towns.

This Tudor shop in Lavenham has a fold-down counter where goods could be displayed when the shop was open. Notice also the peg holes where the timbers were joined together.

Towns and cities where Tudor architecture may be seen.

N

Edinburgh
Berwick-on-Tweed
Lincoln
Chester
King's Lynn
Warwick
Stratford-upon-Avon
Cambridge
Tenby
Burford
Lavenham
Oxford
Singleton

Shopkeepers usually lived above their shops. There were often workshops at the back of the building or weaving looms in the attic.

Many of the town's streets are still made up entirely of Tudor houses built around a wooden frame. The original owners showed off their wealth by using lots of fine timber and leaving it exposed for all to see. The gaps between the timbers were filled with wattle and daub. This was a mixture of mud, cow dung and chopped straw plastered onto sticks wedged between the timbers.

TUDOR HOUSES

Tudor houses are easy to recognise. They are often built from dark oak timbers and pale plaster. Grander houses were sometimes built from brick.

At the Weald and Downland Museum in Sussex, historians have reconstructed a typical Tudor farmhouse. It is called Bayleaf Farmhouse and it has been furnished exactly as it would have been in 1540.

The historians who reconstructed Bayleaf took their evidence from a series of 'inventories'. These are lists of possessions which were made when people died. Thousands of these documents survive in local record offices. They give us a picture of what it was like inside ordinary Tudor homes.

The hall at Bayleaf Farmhouse has no ceiling. This allows smoke from the fire to escape more easily. There are no upstairs rooms in this part of the house.

The hall was the most important room at Bayleaf. Simple Tudor homes like this had no chimneys. The smoke had to find its way out through the unglazed windows or the gaps under the roof. The master and his family would have eaten their meals at the long, oak dining table.

THE DRAUGHT

Tudors called the lavatory 'the draught'. At Bayleaf the lavatory sticks out from the wall of the main bedroom and empties directly into an ash-filled pit below. Using it must have been a draughty experience! The Tudors did not have toilet paper. Instead they used leaves, grass, or little squares of old rag. The first flushing lavatory was invented in 1596 by a Tudor gentleman called Sir John Harrington. He called it his 'Ajax'. The idea never caught on, and it had to be re-invented almost 200 years later!

This Welsh farmhouse was a typical middle-class Tudor home. Such houses usually had two main living rooms called the hall and parlour. Upstairs rooms were used for storage, sleeping and work such as spinning or weaving.

We know that the Tudors found their bedrooms draughty because their beds had curtains all around them. Poor families often had one bed where everyone slept together. At Bayleaf the children had their own little beds in their parents' bedroom.

COUNTRY ESTATES

Some families became very rich under Tudor rule. They bought land and built great houses in the countryside.

Ingatestone Hall in Essex was built for Sir William Petre in 1540. It was very modern for its time, being one of the first houses in England to have piped water and drains.

Ingatestone was designed around two courtyards, a common design in Tudor times. If we visit the Outer Court, we realise that almost everything eaten and drunk by the Petre family was produced on their own estate. The courtyard contained a mill house, a bolting house where flour was sifted, a bake house, a brew house, a fish house, a slaughter house, a buttery and a cheese chamber. There was also a wash house and a room for making candles.

The Petre family's living quarters at Ingatestone. The little tower has stairs in it leading to the bed chambers and attics.

The family's living quarters were built around the Inner Court. Inside the house Sir William's bed can still be seen in the room known as His Lordship's Bedroom. The headboard is carved with his personal coat of arms.

Bramall Hall

Doddington Hall

Hardwick Hall

Oxborough Hall

Burghley House

Ingatestone Hall

Ham House

Cotehele House

N

◀ **Large Tudor homes open to the public.**

There is a priest hole in the house. Catholic priests were persecuted during part of the Tudor period. This hole was used as a secret hiding place. It could only be entered by climbing down the ladder that ran from the trap door in the floor of the room above. Similar priest holes have been found in other Tudor houses.

SANS DIEU RIEN

The arched entrance to the outer courtyard at Ingatestone, where the workshops, stores and servants' quarters were located.

Rich Tudor homes needed many rooms where large numbers of guests and their servants could be accommodated, fed and entertained.

Some houses, like Ingatestone, had a 'long gallery' where people could take exercise, or gather for music, singing and dancing. Feeding up to fifty guests needed careful planning with well-stocked food stores and extra hands to prepare and serve the food.

▼ **The conduit house. Water was piped from here to all parts of Ingatestone Hall.**

FOOD AND COOKING

Tudor writers tell us that there was plenty of good food for the wealthy. They ate several kinds of meat, including peacock and swan. On Fridays it was against the law to eat meat, so everyone ate fish.

▲ The kitchen fireplace at Cotehele was very wide to allow many pots and spits to be heated at the same time.

At Cotehele House in Cornwall you can see a kitchen that has remained almost unchanged since Tudor times. Cotehele was built in the 1480s. By looking at it we can learn a great deal about the kind of food that the Tudors ate, and the ways that it was prepared.

Everything was cooked over an open log fire. Meat was placed on big iron skewers called spits which were held in place by hooks. The rack above the fireplace held spits that were not in use. Pots for making soups and stews were hung from adjustable hooks attached to an iron bar.

There are hooks and racks inside the chimney. These were used to smoke ham over the fire. The hooks would also have been used to dry fish and to store strings of herbs and garlic and sides of salted meat.

The little cupboard to the left of the fire was always warm and dry. This made it ideal for storing salt. Salt was a very important ingredient in the Tudor kitchen. Meat and fish could be stored in salt for long periods.

The vast kitchen at Burghley House in Lincolnshire dates from about 1570. Meals for hundreds of guests were prepared here.

A modern re-enactment of a Tudor banquet performed at Dover Castle in Kent.

TUDOR BANQUETS
Guests were often invited to large houses and palaces to attend banquets. These lavish meals could have as many as ten courses. At a banquet given for Queen Elizabeth I by the Earl of Leicester at Kenilworth, there were 300 different dishes to choose from. At some banquets pastries were served made in the shapes of different animals and even castles.

TUDOR FURNISHINGS

During the Tudor period, life for the rich became more comfortable. Soft feather beds replaced straw mattresses on the floor and hard seats were padded with cushions.

The Tudors built their furnishings, like their houses, out of the toughest oak wood. If you visit Hardwick Hall in Derbyshire you will find that many of the original furnishings made for the house in the 1590s are still in place. Chairs with arms, like the ones in the Great Hall at Hardwick, were reserved for important visitors.

There are many hidden messages for us to find among the decorations at Hardwick. A Tudor visitor entering a great house would look for the owner's coat of arms. Bess of Hardwick, who had Hardwick Hall built, has her coat of arms over the fireplace in the Great Hall.

The Hardwick coat of arms over the fireplace in the Great Hall is very impressive. It is supported by two carved stags.

▼ The ceilings of Tudor rooms were often beautiful. This is a ceiling at Burghley, carved with the date 1577.

'HARDWICK HALL,
MORE GLASS
THAN WALL'
This is a line from a
Tudor rhyme about
Hardwick Hall. Glass
was an expensive luxury
in Tudor times. The
windows at Hardwick
look large to us today.
Imagine how grand they
looked to Tudor eyes!

Many of the walls at Hardwick
are lined with beautiful tapestries.
These were designed to tell us
that the owner was both rich
and educated. In the Great
Chamber there is a colourful
scene in the plaster work. It
shows the Goddess Diana who
has been made to look very like
Queen Elizabeth I. We know
that Bess always hoped to
entertain the Queen here on
one of her many tours, or
'progresses', around the
country, but she never came.

Scenes from Greek or Roman
mythology were popular
subjects for Tudor tapestries.

TUDOR GARDENS

Among the rich, making beautiful gardens became very fashionable. Their style was sometimes copied from the gardens of Italy.

The Moseley knot garden uses different coloured gravels to highlight the shapes in the pattern.

This is the garden of an Elizabethan house called Moseley Old Hall, in Cheshire. The garden is made from hedges and small, carefully clipped trees that have been planted in patterns. The ground is covered with gravel. Gardens like this were called 'knot gardens'.

Knot gardens were very fashionable in Tudor England. This knot garden is quite modern, but it was planted according to a 1640 pattern. This itself was based on a pattern from a gardening book of 1571. Tudor ideas about gardens remained fashionable for a long time.

MAZES

Many Tudor gardens had mazes or labyrinths. These were often laid out in turf. By following the winding path to the centre of the maze, it was possible to take a lot of exercise in a small space. The turf maze provided an amusing entertainment without any risk of getting lost.

Another common feature in Tudor gardens was the mount. This was a small hill, built so that the garden could be seen from a height. The knot garden looked particularly striking when seen from above.

At the Weald and Downland Open Air Museum in Sussex, the garden of an ordinary Tudor farmhouse has been recreated. It is very different from the pleasure gardens of the rich. Most of the work here would have been done by the farmer's wife.

She had to grow enough food for about six adults and the farm servants. She also grew herbs to make medicines and ointments, to use in the kitchen or to strew on the parlour floor.

The Tudor farmhouse garden at the Weald and Downland Museum. The soil would have been enriched with dung from the farmyard.

THE TUDOR NAVY

When Henry VIII came to power, England had only a small navy. During his reign Henry spent a great deal of money building up a large fleet to defend the kingdom.

A modern impression of the *Mary Rose* as it must have looked in 1545.

In 1965, the wreck of a Tudor warship called the *Mary Rose* was discovered in the soft mud beneath Portsmouth harbour. After more than 450 years under water, the ship was brought to the surface. The skeletons of 200 men, their weapons and many of their possessions were found on board. This new evidence tells us a great deal about the lives of Tudor sailors and Tudor defences.

Written records tell us that the *Mary Rose* sank during a battle against the French Navy in 1545. The gun ports were opened and cannons prepared for fire when the ship turned sharply and tipped over. Water rushed through the gun ports and the ship sank almost at once. Only 35 of the 700 people on board survived.

Only the most powerful guns aboard the *Mary Rose* were made of bronze, like this huge cannon called a culverin.

18

These small personal items once belonged to the sailors aboard the *Mary Rose*. They include a comb, a pocket sundial and rosary beads.

Ninety-one guns were found on board the ship. They were all mounted on wheel carriages. This would have allowed the gunners to pull the guns back from the gun ports for cleaning and reloading.

Some of the men on board the *Mary Rose* were archers. There were 138 long bows and 3,500 arrows stowed on the ship. The archers must have been very strong. Pulling a Tudor bow was the equivalent of lifting a 45kg weight.

The crew were equipped with daggers, pikes and hooked blades called bills. This shows that Tudor sailors expected to engage in hand-to-hand fighting with the enemy.

COASTAL FORTS

Henry VIII built 20 forts between Hull and Milford Haven in Wales. Not far from the *Mary Rose*, you can visit Calshott Castle. It would have been packed with gunpowder and equipped with the latest cannons. Its own walls were built to resist gunfire.

PARISH CHURCHES

Until the 1530s, the English Church was ruled by the Pope in Rome. Henry VIII did not like the power the Roman Catholic Church had in Britain.

Eventually Henry VIII broke away from Rome. A new religion developed. The followers of this new religion were called Protestants because they protested against the Roman Catholic Church.

The Protestants objected to some of the old Catholic beliefs and 'reformed' the Church to make worship simpler. This period was called the Reformation. At a time when religion governed people's lives, the Reformation affected everybody. Anyone who refused to change to the new Protestant religion was persecuted.

▼ The rood screen at Attleborough was decorated with coats of arms and pictures of the saints.

The Reformation also brought about changes to the interior decoration of many churches. In Attleborough Church in Norfolk, for example, there is a beautiful painted screen called a rood screen. Before the Reformation rood screens were used to separate the priest from his parishioners. The Protestants did not like this and most screens were destroyed.

The rood screen in Attleborough Church was taken down and hidden. It wasn't found again until quite recently when it was put back in its original position.

On the wall inside Attleborough Church there is a picture of the angel Gabriel telling the Virgin Mary that she will have a baby. Before the Reformation the walls of most churches were decorated with paintings like this. Today, wall paintings are unusual because so many of them were scrubbed off or painted over by the Protestants.

▲ Only parts of the Attleborough wall painting survived damage during the Reformation.

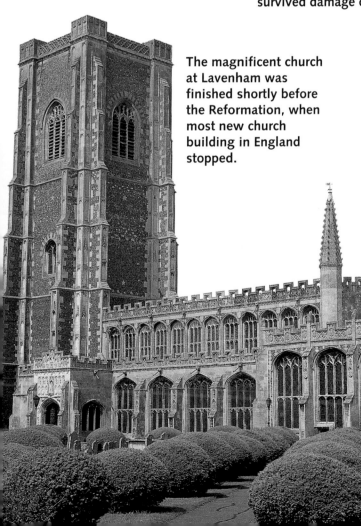

The magnificent church at Lavenham was finished shortly before the Reformation, when most new church building in England stopped.

SUPREME HEAD

When King Henry VIII made himself 'Supreme Head of the Church in England', he ordered the royal coat of arms to be hung in every church. This practice was continued by Henry's children. See if you can find the royal arms in your local church.

Queen Elizabeth I's coat of arms.

21

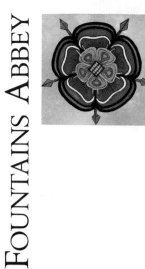

MONASTERIES

In early Tudor times the church was richer than the king himself. Wealthy people often gave land or money to monasteries, so that monks would pray for them after they died.

Most Tudor monasteries are now in ruins, but Fountains Abbey in Yorkshire is one of the better preserved sites. It can help us to find out about the lives led by Tudor monks.

Fountains Abbey has lain in ruins since King Henry VIII ordered it to close in 1539.

Like most monasteries, Fountains was built near a river which provided fresh water and drainage.

This door led up to the readers' desk in the monks' refectory. They were not allowed to speak during meals, so religious books were read to them instead.

Like many other monasteries, Fountains was closed during the reign of Henry Vlll. The King was threatened by the power of the church and jealous of its wealth. In 1534, he declared himself Head of the Church in England.

Soon after, he ordered all monasteries to close. Some, like Norwich, became cathedrals. Others, such as Hexham in Northumberland, became parish churches. Many, like Newstead near Nottingham, became private houses. Most were like Fountains. They were sold, stripped of valuable lead and stone, and left in ruins.

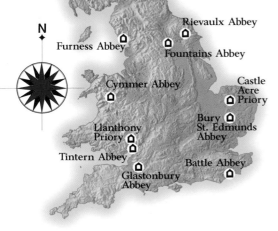

The sites of Tudor monasteries that can be visited today.

Iona Abbey

N

Furness Abbey

Rievaulx Abbey

Fountains Abbey

Cymmer Abbey

Castle Acre Priory

Llanthony Priory

Bury St. Edmunds Abbey

Tintern Abbey

Battle Abbey

Glastonbury Abbey

23

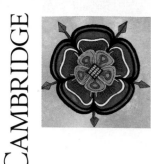

TUDOR EDUCATION

Most children in Tudor times did not go to school. They began work at the age of five or six, usually helping their parents. Some boys went to school, but girls were rarely educated.

A woodcut illustration of a Tudor schoolroom. The master (left) is holding a cane!

Many Tudor villages had a parish school where the local vicar taught boys to read and write. Tudor schoolrooms have survived in places like in Norwich, Winchester and Burford, in Oxfordshire. These rooms show us that Tudor schoolchildren sat in cold, dimly lit and overcrowded classrooms. Two hundred boys were crammed into a single room in Eton's Upper School.

In order to find well-paid work in the church, the law or even royal service, some boys went to university at the age of about fourteen. There were only two universities in Tudor England - Oxford and Cambridge. Today, many students at Cambridge colleges still occupy rooms originally built for Tudor boys.

At Magdalene College, Cambridge, the students eat in the Tudor hall. Above the door of the passage between the hall and the kitchens is the college motto, '*Garde Ta Foy*'. This is French for 'Guard Your Faith'. It reminds us that the universities were mainly used to train people for the church.

Henry VIII needed well-educated men to work for him. The monasteries had been centres for education. When they closed, Henry had to refound many monastic schools, using his own money. This is why there are so many 'King's' schools all over Britain.

▲ The fan-vaulted roof of King's College Chapel, Cambridge is crowned with giant Tudor roses.

KING'S COLLEGE

The chapel of King's College, Cambridge is one of the most beautiful of all Tudor buildings. Magnificent stone carvings decorate the chapel inside and out. The carved coat of arms, crown and Tudor rose were all symbols used by Henry VIII. They remind us that the King himself paid for the chapel to be completed in 1515.

▼ The main court at Magdalene College with its Tudor dining hall, chapel and students' rooms.

ENTERTAINMENT

Tudor people could choose from many different kinds of entertainment. They loved shows with animals in them. The theatre was also very popular.

A performance of Shakespeare's *The Merchant of Venice* at the New Globe Theatre in 1998. The 'groundlings' still have to stand, just like Tudor theatre-goers.

One of the most important theatres in the country opened in London in 1599. It was called The Globe. The famous Tudor playwright William Shakespeare provided some of the money needed to build it and his plays were often performed there.

Until 1989, we could only guess at The Globe's original appearance. Shakespeare referred to it as a 'wooden O' and it was pictured on maps and in pictures of London, but nobody knew how accurate these were.

When a house on the site of the original theatre was demolished, archaeologists uncovered part of The Globe's foundations. To their surprise, they found that it was not circular at all - it had 20 straight sides. Using this evidence, and the study of surviving timber-framed Tudor buildings elsewhere, The Globe theatre was reconstructed. We can be sure that the New Globe Theatre is a very close copy of the original.

The stalls and stage were covered with thatch, but the poorest playgoers, called 'groundlings' or 'stinkards', paid one penny to stand in the open air at the centre of the building.

Archaeologists found many hazelnut shells amongst the remains of The Globe. At first they thought that they had been dropped by nut-chewing theatre-goers. Now they realise that the nutshells, which were mixed with ashes, sand and salt, were to make a well-drained surface for the open floor.

The New Globe Theatre is in Southwark. Plays are only performed here during the summer months.

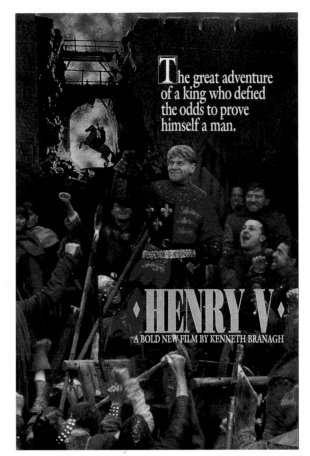

The great adventure of a king who defied the odds to prove himself a man.

HENRY V

A BOLD NEW FILM BY KENNETH BRANAGH

▲ Shakespeare's plays are still popular today. Here is a poster for Kenneth Branagh's film version of *Henry V*.

A GLORIOUS AGE

The Tudors ruled England from 1485 to 1603. Look around you and see what clues you can find on the trail of this very important period in our history.

Look out for Tudor buildings. Rich Tudors built houses that would last and they can still be seen in towns and villages all over the country. There are many big Tudor houses that are open to the public which are well worth visiting.

The strong governments of the Tudor kings and queens brought peace and wealth to the land. Now that there was no need to struggle for survival, many more people had time to learn to read and write. Thousands of books, letters, accounts and legal documents have survived from the Tudor period.

Because of a law passed under King Henry VIII, registers were kept of births, marriages and deaths. This means that even the poorest Tudor person cannot be completely forgotten. Ask in your local museum or library to see if it holds any local Tudor registers.

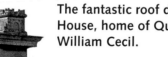

The fantastic roof decorations at Burghley House, home of Queen Elizabeth's secretary, William Cecil.

An Italian-style wall decoration from Burghley.

There are Tudor portraits in galleries, museums and private houses all over Britain. If you can go and look at some of these, you will have some idea of what the Tudors looked like and how they dressed.

Under Tudor rule, English sailors and explorers travelled to new lands. Some of the things that we take for granted today were brought to this country for the first time under the Tudors: potatoes, tobacco, silk and cotton were all new discoveries.

Queen Elizabeth I was the last Tudor monarch. She died in 1603 leaving no heirs, bringing the Tudor dynasty to an end.

Queen Elizabeth's I reign saw a 'great rebuilding of England'. This new gatehouse was added to Stokesay Castle, Shropshire, in 1570.

GLOSSARY

abbey
a place where monks live

archaeologists
people who study the remains
of the past

banquet
a splendid meal for many guests

coat of arms
a shield-shaped badge used by
members of an important family

construction
building or making something

craftsmen
people who are skilled at making
things by hand

demolished
knocked down or destroyed

descendants
the children of our ancestors, later
generations of the same family

fines
money that is paid as a punishment

fort
a small castle

gun ports
holes in a ship's side through which
guns were fired

inventories
lists of people's possessions

loans
money or goods which have been
lent to someone

merchants
people who buy or sell goods

Middle Ages
period of European history from
about 1000 to 1485

portraits
pictures of people

Reformation
when some Christians left the
Catholic church to worship God
in new ways

parishioners
people living locally and attending
the church

persecute
punish because of religious beliefs

'progress'
a long royal journey when the king
or queen stayed with several
important people

prosperous
well-to-do, comfortably off or rich

Protestant
someone who objected to the beliefs
of the Roman Catholic Church and
chose to worship God under the
Protestant religion

registers
official records or lists of names

royal coffers
chests where the king's or the queen's
money was stored

tapestry
a woven wall-hanging

taxes
money which people pay to the
government to run the country

trade
buying and selling goods

wattle and daub
sticks and mud used to fill spaces in
timber-framed buildings

wealth
riches, money

weavers
people who make cloth by weaving it
on a loom

TIMELINE

1485	Henry Tudor wins the Battle of Bosworth and becomes king. Start of Tudor times
1485-1509	Reign of King Henry VII
1509-1547	Reign of King Henry VIII
1534	King Henry VIII breaks with the Pope and becomes Head of the Church in England
1535	The first Bible printed in English is placed in churches
1536-1540	All monasteries are closed and their possessions sold off by the King
1545	The *Mary Rose* sinks in Portsmouth harbour
1547-1553	The reign of King Edward VI. Many new schools and colleges founded
1553-1558	Reign of Queen Mary Tudor
1558-1603	Reign of Queen Elizabeth I
1588	The Spanish Armada is defeated by the English fleet
1599	The Globe theatre opens
1603	Queen Elizabeth I dies. King James of Scotland becomes the first Stuart king of England. End of Tudor times

PLACES TO VISIT

Berwick-on-Tweed: Northumberland - massive Tudor town walls and castle ruins

Burford, Oxfordshire: stone Tudor houses, shops, grammar school and church

Cambridge: university colleges, many built in Tudor times

Chester, Cheshire: rows of fine Elizabethan houses and shops

Edinburgh, Scotland: Huntly House, Gladstone's End and other fine, sixteenth-century houses

King's Lynn, Norfolk: Tudor houses, shops and college

Lincoln: Tudor houses near the cathedral

Oxford: houses, churches and university colleges

Stratford-upon-Avon, Warwickshire: timber-framed Tudor buildings

Tenby, Dyfed, Wales: castle ruins and town buidlings

Warwick: castle and Tudor houses

INDEX